Wise...
and Not So Wise
Ten Tales from the Rabbis

This volume is dedicated
in loving honor of the
birth
of
Deborah Shoshanah Katz
daughter of
Joanne Louise Cohen
and Aaron David Katz
April 9, 2003
by
Goldie (ז״ל) and Abram Cohen (זײל)
Betty Ann (זײל) and D. Walter Cohen
Josephine Cohen
Amy Sue Cohen
Jane and Martin Millner
Rachel, Lauren and Michael Millner

Wise...
and Not So Wise
Ten Tales from the Rabbis

Selected and Retold by Phillis Gershator
Designed and Illustrated by Alexa Ginsburg

The Jewish Publication Society
Philadelphia
2004 • 5764

The Jewish Publication Society
2100 Arch Street
Philadelphia, PA 19103

Design and composition by Alexa Ginsburg
Manufactured in the United States of America

04 05 06 07 08 09 10   10 9 8 7 6 5 4 3 2 1

Library of Congress Cataloging-in-Publication Data
Gershator, Phillis.
Wise and not so wise: ten tales from the rabbis/ selected and retold by Phillis Gershator;
llustrated by Alexa Ginsburg.-- 1st ed.
p. cm.
ISBN 0-8276-0755-5
1. Legends, Jewish. 2. Talmud--Legends. 3. Midrash--Legends. I. Ginsburg, Alexa. II.
Title
BM530.G428 2004
296.1'9--dc22

2004002751

To Bruce Black for suggesting this collection of tales,
to Janet Greenstein Potter for helping me tell them,
and to David, as always—PG

Contents

About these tales . . .
So Many Questions

In days of old, the spoken wisdom of the great
rabbis was gathered together over hundreds of years by
hundreds of teachers. They wrote down everything they
remembered and everything they knew so that it would
never be forgotten. Then, no matter where the people
of Israel lived, they could take their sacred writings with
them. Two of the works the rabbis produced were the
Talmud and the Midrash.

People turned to the Talmud for answers to questions—
about the Torah and about law, medicine, arithmetic,
astronomy, and, most important, how to practice Judaism,
how to become a better person, and how to live a
worthwhile and wholesome life. Today, parents all over
the world continue to pass the teachings of the Talmud
on to their children. And some children, as early as the
age of eight, begin to study the Talmud for themselves.

In the Midrash, people could find the words of
rabbinical scholars, who looked deeply into the Bible to
better understand its meaning. The rabbis drew on their
own experience and the teachings of the sages to answer
questions, teach moral lessons, and even entertain. For
a thousand years, scholars added to this body of work,
which offers a rich source of discussion and magical
wisdom. Nowadays, some poets, writers, and rabbis still
create works in the midrashic style, to explain sacred lore
in new ways for new times.

Inspired by my husband's father—who told me
midrashic and talmudic tales he remembered from
his youth and his studies with Rabbi Abraham Isaac
Kook—I took my first dip in the Talmud, "the sea of
Jewish knowledge." In it I found my favorite treasure:
more stories! The stories contained lessons, truths, jokes,
surprises, happy endings, and many, many questions. And
the questions were answered in many ways—with words,
with silence, with deeds, sometimes with more questions.

For this book, I selected seven tales from the Talmud
and three midrashic tales with a talmudic flavor. The
stories I chose made me laugh or they touched me with
their messages and miracles. I asked some questions
about them, too, wishing that my husband's father, the
late Rabbi Abraham Gershator, were here to help me ask

the right ones. Maybe you, dear reader, will help—and join me in asking and answering, answering and asking, in the great talmudic tradition.

As I retold these tales, I couldn't help stretching and twisting them a little and adding a little more dialogue, which is what storytellers like to do. Most of all, storytellers like to share, so let us share them now— 10 timeless tales of angels, goats, and the wisest of the wise.

Let the stories begin!

Making It Rain

4

No one could pray for rain like Honi the Circle Maker.

When the wells were low and the rain barrels dry, people begged him, "Pray for rain, Honi. Pray for rain." And he prayed: "God, have mercy. Let the rain fall."

If no rain fell, he drew a circle on the ground and stood in the middle of it. Boldly he'd cry, "God, I will not move from this circle until the first drop falls."

God loved Honi like a son, and the rain fell.

Though Honi's children dared not pray for rain with such boldness, they were wise and good children and their quiet prayers were often answered. They, too, became known as rainmakers, and in times of drought, their rainmaking powers were put to the test.

One year, two wise men, whose own prayers didn't work, looked for one of Honi's descendants to pray for rain. They found Abba Hilkiah, Honi's grown-up grandson, working in a farmer's field of grain.

They called out, "Peace be with you, Abba Hilkiah. What are you doing?"

Abba did not pause. He kept pulling weeds from around the rain-starved crops.

The wise men looked at one another and shook their heads, puzzled. Surely he had heard them. Why didn't he answer?

When Abba finished weeding, he gathered up some kindling, and with the wood on his shoulder and his shoes in his hand, he walked home barefoot. The wise men followed.

Before Abba crossed the nearly dried-up riverbed, he stopped and put on his shoes.

The wise men looked at one another and shook their heads, puzzled. Surely Abba had been carrying his shoes to keep them clean. Why was he putting them on to walk through the mud?

When they reached Abba's house, the wise men followed him through the door. Now they could ask him to pray for rain. But Abba did not give them a chance. Instead, he busied himself

serving his two sons their dinner. He gave his firstborn son one portion and his younger son two portions.

The wise men looked at one another and shook their heads, puzzled. Surely the older child needs more food than the younger. Why was Abba so unfair?

Before the men could speak, Abba called his wife to go with him up to the roof.

The wise men looked at one another. They shook their heads, more puzzled than ever. Why did Abba want to go up to the roof? He was acting in such an odd way, they didn't know what to think. But they followed him.

The wise men climbed up the ladder to the roof and stuck their heads out. They saw Abba standing on one corner of the roof, praying. His

wife stood on the opposite corner, also praying. From the corner where Abba's wife stood, with her hands raised to the heavens, a cloud appeared. It grew bigger and blacker, until it covered the sky for miles and the rain began to fall. Abba and his wife climbed back down the ladder.

At last, Abba greeted the wise men. "Welcome to my house," he said. "Thank you for waiting for me so patiently. What can I do for you?"

"Abba Hilkiah, we came to ask you to pray for rain."

Abba said, "You have no need to ask. Behold, it is already raining! Blessed be the Almighty who has made it unnecessary for you to ask a favor of Abba Hilkiah!"

"Yes, we watched you pray for rain. We watched you all day, in fact. And we wondered why you had been acting in such an odd way. Will you tell us why?"

"I will try," Abba said.

"First," one of the wise men asked, "why did you ignore us when we called to you in the field?"

"I had been paid to work," Abba said. "I was not paid to talk. If I had talked with you, I would have had to stop working. Would that have been fair to the man who pays me?"

"Hmm, you may be right, Abba," said one of the wise men after he thought about it. "But that is not the only odd thing. Why did you carry your shoes to keep them clean, then put them on to walk through the mud?"

"In this drought," Abba replied, "all manner of creatures gather wherever there is a drop of water. I wore my shoes to protect myself from scorpions and deadly snakes. Is life not more important than clean shoes?"

"Oh, yes! You are right, Abba, but that is not the only odd thing. Why did you give your youngest son more food than the eldest?"

"The eldest was working in the yard. He could come inside and eat whenever he was hungry. The youngest was at school studying and he had not eaten all day. Should the student be deprived?"

"No, no, of course not! Now you have explained everything! Thank you, Abba, you are indeed the wisest of wise men."

"But you have not asked me the most important question of all," said Abba. "You did not ask me why I asked my wife to pray for rain."

So they asked in one voice, "Why did you ask your wife to pray for rain?"

"Because my wife is the one who does good works. See her there, preparing food for the poor? Now you know the answer to your question. The Almighty loves her and hears her prayers first, before hearing mine."

The wise men left Abba's house wiser than before. All their questions had been answered, including the ones they did not think to ask.

The Talmud has two versions, written in different countries and centuries. One version is called the Jerusalem Talmud. The other one—about four times bigger—is called the Babylonian Talmud. In adapting this story from the Babylonian Talmud (*Ta'anit,* 23a–23b), I chose four of the eight incidents about Abba Hilkiah's puzzling behavior.

Abba Hilkiah, grandson of Honi the Circle Maker, lived in the first century C.E. Although he was meek and shy and labored every day for his wages, he was considered a sage and a miracle worker, like his grandfather before him. And just like his grandfather, he was willing to pray for rain during a drought. So why didn't he want the wise men to ask him to pray? Could he have had a good reason, as he had for everything else he did?

Maybe he had more than one reason—just as rain has more than one name. In the Land of Israel there is the first rain, *yoreh,* and the last rain, *malkosh,* also called early rain and late rain. Without rain, the land would be barren. Nothing would grow or bloom. It's no wonder prayers for rain were so important and rainmakers like Abba Hilkiah were held in such high esteem.

Figs for Gold

Emperor Hadrian, traveling through the lands of Judea, saw an old man contentedly working in his little garden.

He thought out loud, "It is very hard to be emperor. I have so much work to do and everyone wants to tell me how to do it. Here is a man, working hard, and no one is telling him what to do or how to do it. Yet he gets his work done."

He called out to the gardener, "What is the secret of your success, old man?"

"I pick the weeds out one by one, by the roots."

"Ah, yes!" exclaimed the emperor. "That is the secret! One by one! I will solve my problems one by one, not all of them at once. I will listen to my advisors one by one, not all of them at once. I will defeat my enemies one by one, not all of them at once."

The emperor, appreciating the old man's wisdom, gave him a basket of gold.

When the old man's rich and greedy neighbor saw the basket of gold, he ran over, asking, "Neighbor, why did the emperor give you a basket of gold?"

"He liked my garden."

The rich man looked at the little garden, with its pomegranate tree and roses in bloom. The rich man said to himself, "Gold is being handed out. There is no reason I cannot receive some, too. My garden is much bigger." He was too lazy to do the work himself, so he hired a boy to clean up his garden for him and plant a few rosebushes.

Next time the emperor passed, the rich man blocked his way. He bowed and said, "My Master, you love the sight of a beautiful garden. Observe

this garden. It is larger and more beautiful than my neighbor's garden. It is worth at least *two* baskets of gold."

The emperor didn't stop. He pressed his powerful horse forward, knocking the rich man into the dust. The man looked around to see if anyone had noticed, but his neighbor had eyes only for his own work. The old man was digging a hole.

The rich man brushed the dust off his clothes. Then he went and told his wife, "Our neighbor is digging a hole in his garden."

"Old Graybeard's probably going to bury his treasure," she said.

"No, I think he's planting a fig tree."

"How ridiculous! He's so old. He'll never live to enjoy the fruit. What a waste of time. And he'll never live to spend all that gold, either," she said regretfully. "We could have used it faster and better than he ever will."

The emperor, returning the following day, saw the old man planting a small fig tree in the big hole he had dug. He halted his horse and asked, "In your old age, why do you still labor so? Trees take years and years to grow and bear fruit. Do you honestly expect to eat the figs from your tree?"

The old man replied, "If it is the will of God, I shall eat the fruit of the tree. If not, my children shall enjoy it."

The emperor rode away, glancing back for one last look at the old man bent over the young tree.

Emperor Hadrian went on to wage wars. In three years, his empire had grown, extending from sea to sea. At the same time, the little tree grew taller and wider. And the old man had lived to grow three years older, long enough to see the tree's first figs!

When Hadrian chanced to pass that way again, the old man offered him a basket of fat purple figs.

"My Master," said the old man, "you may remember this basket. I am the gardener you spoke to three years ago. Be good enough to receive this gift—fruit from my fig tree."

Hadrian did remember the basket, and he hadn't forgotten the wise old man and his garden either. He returned the basket, once again filled with gold.

The rich man's wife saw her neighbor with a basket of gold. Curiosity—and greed—made her ask, "Neighbor, where did you get all that gold?"

"From the emperor," he replied. "He liked the fruit I gave him."

She immediately told her husband, "Graybeard gave the emperor a basket of fruit and received a basket of gold in return. Quick, run out and buy some fruit. Since the emperor loves the fruit of this land so much, he'll reward you, too, and fill your basket with gold."

The rich man went to the marketplace to buy fruit, but he could find nothing to match his neighbor's fresh figs, even though he had plenty of money to spend.

So that night, he crept over the wall and stole the last figs from the old man's tree, telling himself, "Old Graybeard won't miss a few figs. He'll think the birds ate them. Anyway, if the old

fellow lived this long, he'll surely live a little longer. It's not as though his tree won't bear fruit again next year. And look, his pomegranates are almost ripe."

He kept talking to himself, but no matter what he said, he still knew he was doing something he should not do, and in his haste to get away and climb back over the wall, he tripped and fell. The greedy man twisted his ankle.

A basket of gold is worth the pain, he thought.

Next morning, he took the gift of fruit to the emperor's camp. Granted permission to speak to the emperor, he limped forward and handed Hadrian the fruit.

"My Master, I have heard how fond you are of the fruit of our land. Fresh figs like these can't be found in any market."

"Thank you. But you appear bruised. You're limping as though you've been to war."

"Oh, I tripped and fell off my neighbor's wall. But as you can see, the fruit wasn't bruised at all. If you don't mind, I'll take the gold now and go home and soak my foot."

The emperor was angry. Not only was the man greedy, but he had stolen the fruit! And now he expected a reward!

The emperor handed the basket to his guards and gave orders that every purple fig be returned to the thief, one by one.

The guards threw the figs, one by one, splattering the rich man with skin, seeds, and juice until he ran off in disgrace.

Back home, hobbling through the door, he was greeted by his wife: "Where's the gold?"

"Where's the gold?" he repeated. "Ask the emperor's guards. They pelted me with Graybeard's figs. And after all the trouble I went to! Oh, my aching ankle. I could hardly run. It's lucky Graybeard's pomegranates weren't ripe yet. Imagine if I had taken the emperor a basket of pomegranates. Pomegranates are as hard as rocks!"

In "Figs for Gold," Hadrian—the Roman emperor who ruled from 117 to 138 C.E.—rewards a wise and generous Jew. Yet in other stories (see "Teacher in a Cave"), Hadrian is the oppressor. How can that be?

At first, Hadrian was considered an enlightened monarch who cared about the well-being of his subjects. But as his reign progressed, his actions inflamed the people of Judea, which was then a Roman province. In 70 C.E., the Romans had destroyed the Second Temple. In 130 C.E., Hadrian decided to build a Roman temple on that sacred Jewish site. His plan, and the oppressive rules and restrictions he had imposed on the people, ignited a revolt led by the popular Jewish warrior known as Bar Kochba. Hadrian launched a massive counterattack. He savagely persecuted the Israelites in his attempt to crush their religion and spirit of independence, and he succeeded in building his temple.

"Figs for Gold" has its origin in a section of the Midrash, called *Va-yikra Rabbah,* 25:5, compiled in the fifth century C.E. The ancient rabbis told midrashim—tales and parables—to explain and interpret the Bible and, later on, the Talmud. Talmudic and midrashic folklore usually teach moral lessons, sometimes with a dash of humor. Would this story be amusing if we didn't know the difference between right and wrong? How do we learn the difference in the first place? Would Emperor Hadrian make a good teacher?

Hanina's Stone

What a beautiful city!" cried the rabbi. "Stone towers! Stone gates! Stone walls!"

The city of pink-and-gold stone was Jerusalem, and the awestruck rabbi was Hanina Ben Dosa.

Hanina was not only a rabbi. He was a stone-cutter. To keep bread on the table, he worked hard at his trade. Even then, he was poor, very poor, and he and his wife sometimes went without bread. But for Hanina, a longed-for trip to Jerusalem was more important than bread.

Now, in Jerusalem for the first time, he marveled, his eyes wide, at the stones of Jerusalem's towers, gates, and walls. The biggest stones were as tall as a man, as wide as a house!

When Hanina saw the Temple itself, high on its platform above the huge stone walls, he could hardly believe his eyes. The Temple was made of marble and gold. It glittered in the sun like a snow-covered mountain.

Hanina walked up the wide stairway to the Temple. He saw people bringing offerings—animals, food, silver, gold … .

Everyone has brought an offering, he realized, *and I have none. How will I show my respect?*

Empty-handed, he left slowly, dragging his feet, wanting with all his heart to turn around and climb that stairway once more—if only he could think of a suitable offering to bring with him.

Outside the city, he sat upon a stone to rest. The stone was a piece of long, wide limestone, pink and gold, the color of dawn. It was a comfortable seat, not too high, not too low.

Hanina sat quietly on the stone, watching the ants trek through the tall grass. They carried bits of leaves many times their size.

A wonderful idea came to him: *This very stone will be my offering! I will shape it, chisel it smooth, and bring it to Jerusalem. Tired visitors like myself can sit on it and rest and gaze upon the Temple glittering in the sun. It would be a good deed! God welcomes good deeds!*

Hanina took out the stonecutting tools he always carried in his bag and began to clean the stone.

The stone was heavy. Its weight did not stop Hanina from working on it, cleaning, shaping, cutting, and then polishing the stone until it glowed. But when he was finished, no matter how hard he tried, Hanina could not move it in the direction of Jerusalem, not one inch.

How could I have dared to think I could ever be as strong as an ant? he asked himself.

Hanina tried to hire a wagon and driver to take the stone to Jerusalem, but he had only five coins. No one would help him for only five coins. The people who passed by said, "Five coins is not enough to hire one workman, let alone a wagon and driver."

Hanina sat on his stone, thinking: *What shall I do now? What shall I do with my offering? I can't carry it all by myself to Jerusalem.*

Hanina, the stonecutting rabbi, called out to the Almighty. "I cut the stone with all my skill. The stone is as beautiful as any in Jerusalem, but now I can't take it there. Is it that my good deed was greater than my wisdom? Even five strong men couldn't carry such a big stone!"

As he thought those thoughts and said those words, five strong men appeared before him.

Hanina stared, blinking—thinking that the bright overhead sun had affected his sight. But he quickly gathered his wits. "Would you help me carry this stone to Jerusalem?" he asked. Then he paused, adding, "Unfortunately, I can pay you only five coins for your trouble. That is all I have."

"That is enough, as long as you help," said the strongest of the five strong men.

At the count of three, all six men lifted the stone.

Clouds surrounded them. A dark cloud hovered overhead, protecting them from the hot sun. A shining cloud led the way so they would not stumble. A powerful cloud pressed them from behind, like wind in the sails of a boat.

The clouds lifted once they reached Jerusalem. There, the men tenderly placed the stone within sight of the Temple. Hanina counted out his last five coins. When he looked up to pay his helpers, they had disappeared.

What happened? How could five strong men vanish in an instant? he wondered.

As soon as Hanina returned to his home in the Galilee, he told his wife the whole story.

"My deed was greater than my wisdom," he concluded.

"Yes, your deed was greater than your wisdom," she agreed, "but the Almighty was pleased. And that is why those men came along.

"No, not men," she corrected herself, realizing that her husband's pleasing deed had been followed by a miracle.

"They were angels," she said. "God sent angels to help you!"

This story is originally from the Midrash, *Kohelet Rabbah,* 1:1, written in the eighth century c.e. It illustrates one of Hanina Ben Dosa's lessons: "All those whose deeds are more than their wisdom, their wisdom endures; all who please mankind with their deeds also please God." Reading his words, we understand why this poor and pious rabbi was known for preferring silent prayer to flowery speeches, and action over talk. In his own prayers and deeds, he attempted to achieve the impossible—and he did so, according to legendary tales like this one.

Is it foolish to dream and then work to make the dream come true, however impractical that dream may be? Rabbi Hanina would say that if the dream is a worthy one, pursuing it is the opposite of foolishness. But why, then, is it a *wise* thing to do? Can good deeds, even if they defy common sense, inspire others? Can they inspire the angels?

According to the Midrash, when Hanina related the story of his helpers to the members of the Sanhedrin—the Jewish high council—the court responded, "Indeed, it seems to us that God sent angels to help you." In my version, Hanina's wife is the one to reach that conclusion.

"Hanina's Stone" is the first of three stories in this book featuring Rabbi Hanina and his wife. They lived in the first century C.E., but we don't know exactly when they died—whether before or after the beautiful Second Temple was destroyed. But surely the rabbi's stone is still there, somewhere in the pink-and-gold city of Jerusalem.

Teacher in
the Cave

In ancient times, Hadrian, the Roman emperor, ruled the Land of Israel. He commanded those he ruled to forget their Hebrew ways, to do as the Romans did and believe as the Romans believed.

"The Roman way is the right way. It is the only way," declared Hadrian. "Praise the new!"

Some Israelites refused to praise the new and forget the old.

Instead, in order to keep the study of their traditional beliefs and teachings alive, they sent their children to Shimon Bar Yohai's school. Shimon Bar Yohai was such a brilliant rabbi he could answer one question with 24 answers.

When Hadrian discovered his orders had been disobeyed, he was furious. "Arrest Shimon Bar Yohai!" he commanded his soldiers.

At that same moment, a bird flew into Bar Yohai's house. It flapped its wings and chirped loudly.

"What is this little bird trying to say?" wondered the rabbi. "It seems frightened. It wants to fly, but it chirps as though it wants me to fly, too."

The rabbi spoke to the bird. "Am I to follow you, little bird?" The bird flew around the room, chirping even louder, and Bar Yohai knew, as his eyes followed the circling bird, that he must follow. The rabbi's son, Eleazar, joined him.

The bird led the way up into the hills, to a cave hidden among the sandy, rocky slopes. In the distance, they heard the tramp, tramp, tramp of Hadrian's soldiers.

"The soldiers are after us!" Bar Yohai cried. "The bird warned us to flee just in time. A miracle! And it led us to a cave where we can hide.

Another miracle! Though we have no food and no water here in the hills," he told his son, "we are still alive, and for that, let us give thanks."

The bird returned before dark with a shiny brown seed in its beak. It dropped the seed near the cave.

At once, the seed sprouted.

Overnight, beneath the bright moon, the sprout grew into a carob tree. Father and son awoke in the morning to find ripe carobs hanging from its branches.

No sooner had they eaten when they heard the sound of water. A spring had appeared in the bone-dry earth. Clear, cool water bubbled up to quench their thirst. Another miracle!

"We will hide here until it is safe to go home," said Bar Yohai. "With food and water and our Bible, we will survive."

✕

Back in the village, the rabbi's young students looked for him.

"The rabbi followed a bird into the hills," a neighbor told the children, "but be careful. The soldiers must never find out where he's hiding, or his life will be in danger."

The children climbed up into the hills. They carried baskets of food. Bows and arrows were slung across their shoulders. They were going hunting—for their teacher! But if a soldier saw them, they could point to their weapons and say, "We're hunting for birds."

On one sandy, rocky slope, they saw a carob tree dripping with ripe brown carobs. "Look! Carobs! Let's pick them."

The rabbi heard familiar voices. They were the voices of his students, picking carobs right outside his cave!

"My children!" he cried.

"Bar Yohai, Bar Yohai, Rabbi Bar Yohai!" they shouted. "We found you! Now you will be our teacher again!"

Bar Yohai was so happy he danced around and around, singing, "The children will learn. The children will remember. The teachings of old will not be lost!"

⋊⋉

Each week the children went off to the hills with their baskets and their bows and arrows, keeping a sharp lookout for soldiers. They didn't want to reveal Bar Yohai's hiding place.

One day, the children, all except Jacob, the oldest, were sitting with the rabbi in his cave. Jacob was outside, up in the tree picking carobs, when a band of soldiers passed by.

"What are you doing here, boy?" a soldier asked, looking up in the tree.

"P-p-p-picking carobs," he answered, scared. Then he spoke louder, as a warning to the others in the cave. "WOULD YOU SOLDIERS LIKE SOME CAROBS?"

Abram heard Jacob shouting "CAROBS." Thinking his brother needed help picking carobs, he ran out of the cave. But when he saw the soldiers, he stopped short.

"Are you frightened, Abram?" Jacob said loudly. "I told you not to go into that cave. It might be full of BATS and RATS and DEADLY SCORPIONS. Maybe even POISONOUS SNAKES.

You should listen to me next time," he warned. "Now come here and give these hungry soldiers some carobs."

Abram brought carobs to the soldiers. "I was frightened in the cave," he explained. "Bats and rats and scorpions …"

"I hate rats," one of the soldiers said.

"So do I," said another soldier. "I hate scorpions, too. And snakes. Let's get out of here!"

Once the soldiers were gone, Bar Yohai himself ran outside to hug the children. "Bless you!" he cried. "You saved my life! You and a little bird."

Bar Yohai and Eleazar hid in the cave for 12 years. At the end of the 12th year, Bar Yohai heard a loud chirping outside his cave. He saw a bird struggling to escape from a net, but before he could release it the bird flew free.

"This is a sign," Bar Yohai announced, "a sign we can go home again. We're free now, like the bird."

He was right. Hadrian had died and the soldiers were gone, leaving teachers free to teach Torah and their students free to learn.

Shimon Bar Yohai was a second-century sage and famous teacher. His death in 160 C.E. occurred 33 days after Pesach, on Lag ba-Omer. Today, many people go up to Meron in the Galilee, where Bar Yohai once lived, to honor him and to celebrate the holiday of Lag ba-Omer with picnics, bonfires, and songs.

According to the Babylonian Talmud (*Shabbat,* 33b), when Bar Yohai escaped from the Roman authorities, a bountiful carob tree and bubbling spring helped saved his life. To these miracles, I added a new incident to the story, though not a miraculous one—Jacob and the Roman soldiers.

In the Talmud, Bar Yohai's story doesn't stop with Hadrian's death. The story continues: After 12 years in his cave, Bar Yohai came to believe that his way was the only way and that the study of Torah was life's only important occupation. Leaving his cave at last, he saw farmers toiling in their fields. He looked upon the scene with such scorching anger that his burning glance set the farmers' crops on fire. At once, Bar Yohai heard a voice from the heavens cry, "Did you come out of there to destroy the world? Return to your cave!"

Had Bar Yohai become as intolerant as the Romans? In this tale, we learn about intolerance and the constant battle we must wage against it—even in ourselves. We learn, too, that people can change. Bar Yohai obeyed God's voice and returned to his cave—and he emerged again one year later, wiser than before. Yet no matter how wise someone may be, can any one person know what's right for everyone else?

Can any one person have all the answers?

Goats for
Chickens

46

A traveler left two scrawny chickens with Rabbi Hanina Ben Dosa and his wife.

"I'll only be gone a short while," he said, "but I don't want my chickens to run away while I'm gone."

"Don't worry," said Hanina's wife. "We'll keep your two chickens in the house. We won't let them run away."

Hanina's wife lovingly tended to the chickens. They grew shiny and plump and, happily clucking louder than ever, they laid a batch of eggs.

"Don't use the eggs," Hanina warned his wife. "Those eggs belong to the owner of the chickens."

Months passed. The traveler still hadn't returned. Meanwhile, the eggs hatched and the chicks grew. The hens among them laid eggs, and the proud roosters crowed.

47

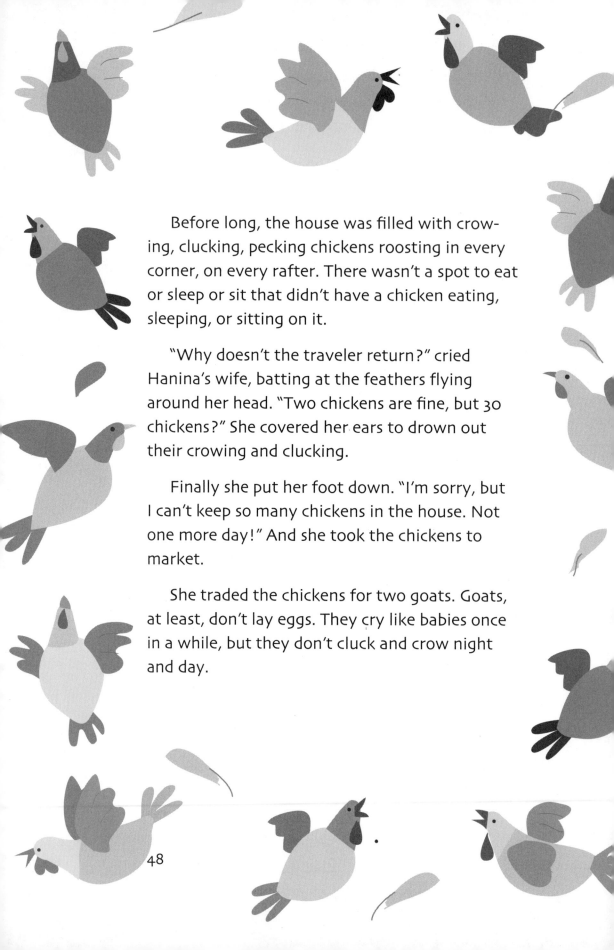

Before long, the house was filled with crow-ing, clucking, pecking chickens roosting in every corner, on every rafter. There wasn't a spot to eat or sleep or sit that didn't have a chicken eating, sleeping, or sitting on it.

"Why doesn't the traveler return?" cried Hanina's wife, batting at the feathers flying around her head. "Two chickens are fine, but 30 chickens?" She covered her ears to drown out their crowing and clucking.

Finally she put her foot down. "I'm sorry, but I can't keep so many chickens in the house. Not one more day!" And she took the chickens to market.

She traded the chickens for two goats. Goats, at least, don't lay eggs. They cry like babies once in a while, but they don't cluck and crow night and day.

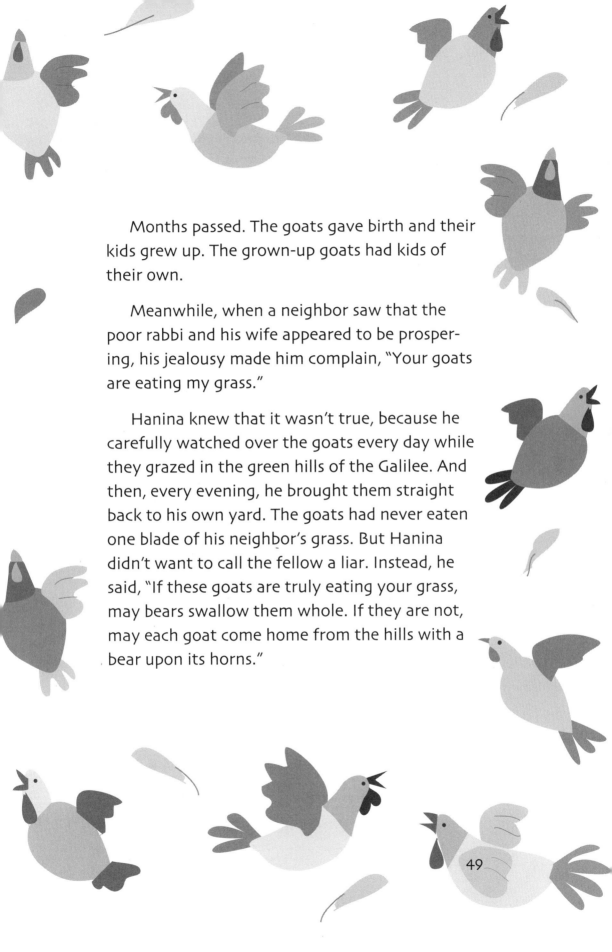

Months passed. The goats gave birth and their kids grew up. The grown-up goats had kids of their own.

Meanwhile, when a neighbor saw that the poor rabbi and his wife appeared to be prospering, his jealousy made him complain, "Your goats are eating my grass."

Hanina knew that it wasn't true, because he carefully watched over the goats every day while they grazed in the green hills of the Galilee. And then, every evening, he brought them straight back to his own yard. The goats had never eaten one blade of his neighbor's grass. But Hanina didn't want to call the fellow a liar. Instead, he said, "If these goats are truly eating your grass, may bears swallow them whole. If they are not, may each goat come home from the hills with a bear upon its horns."

That evening, just before sundown, the villagers beheld an astonishing sight: a flock of goats trotting home, each one with a bear upon its horns!

✕

The traveler returned at long last. "Where are my chickens?" he asked.

The chickens he had left behind were gone, so Hanina and his wife gave him the goats.

Two scrawny chickens for a flock of fat and frisky goats? The traveler was well pleased, except for one nagging, greedy thought.

What if I had stayed away another year? he wondered. *What might have awaited me then? If the rabbi's wife can turn two chickens into a flock of goats, she could turn a flock of goats into a herd of cattle!*

Mourning his loss, the traveler was sorry he'd come home so soon.

Though poor, Rabbi Hanina Ben Dosa was so honest he wouldn't even eat the eggs from someone else's chickens. Yet he was accused of allowing his goats to eat his neighbor's grass. The accusation was as absurd as goats carrying bears on their horns!

There are many folktales in which wealth is achieved by trading up—one small item for a bigger one, until, in the end, the hero or heroine gains the biggest prize of all. In this tale, the rabbi and his wife receive nothing for their cleverness and hard work—not a single egg. What's more, the greedy, stay-away traveler is the one who profits. And what's worse, the rabbi is blamed for something he didn't do.

The strange miracle of the bears and goats makes us stop and think about fairness. Rabbi Hanina often receives God's favor, but it seems as though, despite everything, this miracle leaves him with nothing—or does it leave him with something he might have otherwise lost?

In this story from the Babylonian Talmud (*Ta'anit,* 25a) we never do find out what happened to the bears. Could they have vanished, like angels in disguise?

Everything for the Best

In ancient Rome, authorities outlawed the religious teachings of a famous rabbi, Akiva Ben Yosef. But Rabbi Akiva disobeyed the Romans. He continued to teach.

Astride his donkey, as he traveled from town to town, he always looked on the bright side. He trusted that everything would happen for the best and no soldiers would arrest him.

Traveling light, with only a lamp to study by and a rooster to wake him, the rabbi depended on strangers for shelter. One night, he reached a village where not a single villager offered him a bed. How could it be for the best that the old rabbi was forced to sleep outdoors in an open field?

"Everything God does is for the best," said the rabbi, lying on his back, marveling at the brightness of the stars. "Here I can observe the sky. How beautiful is the glory of the Lord! The skies proclaim the heavens above!"

The wind blew his lamp out, but the rabbi said, "Everything God does is for the best. The stars are so much brighter in the darkness!"

A spotted leopard jumped out from behind a rock and snatched Rabbi Akiva's rooster.

The rabbi sighed, but still he said, "Everything God does is for the best. The leopard must eat to survive, like all God's creatures."

At the sight of the hungry leopard, Rabbi Akiva's donkey ran away.

"Everything God does is for the best," said the rabbi. "If the donkey hadn't run, the leopard might have eaten him, too."

When Rabbi Akiva awoke, he traveled on by foot to the next village, where he learned that Roman soldiers had crossed the field where he'd slept and ransacked the village where he hadn't slept.

Since the rabbi always looked on the bright side, what did he say?

"Everything God does is for the best!

"If, on the one hand, the villagers had been hospitable, the soldiers would have found me.

"If, on the other hand, my lamp had not blown out, my rooster had not been eaten, and my donkey had not run away, the soldiers would have been led by lamp's light, rooster's crow, and donkey's bray to my bed of weeds.

"And then," he said, raising both hands to the sky, "poor Akiva would no longer be free to say, again and again, 'Everything God does is for the best!'"

Rabbi Akiva Ben Yosef lived in the first and second centuries (50–135 C.E.) and was a renowned scholar and teacher. This story from the Babylonian Talmud (*Berachot,* 60b) tells us a little about Rabbi Akiva's character. He was revered for his learning and loved for his simplicity and devotion to the people.

Akiva lived during a time of strife and persecution. He even witnessed the destruction of much of the city of Jerusalem. Yet he was hopeful and optimistic. When saying "Everything is for the best," he was repeating a belief that he had learned in school, and he handed that positive point of view down to his own students.

As an old man, Rabbi Akiva was imprisoned by the Romans for teaching Torah, but he kept on teaching, even in jail. He is one of 10 martyrs whose murders are recalled in the Yom Kippur prayer, *Eleh Ezkerah*—"These I shall remember."

Today, when things go badly for us, how do we keep our spirits up? Do we observe that a glass is half full instead of half empty? Do we ever say, like Rabbi Akiva, that everything is for the best? How can we truly believe it? How can *everything* be for the best?

What's Cooking?

Though it was said that Hanina Ben Dosa could work miracles, he never changed poor people into rich ones—not even himself and his wife, who were very, very poor. They were so poor, often they didn't even have bread for the Sabbath.

On those Fridays when Rabbi Hanina's wife had no flour to bake bread, she baked twigs in the oven instead.

"The neighbors will see smoke rising out of the chimney," she told herself. "They will think I'm baking bread. Then no one will feel sorry for us, and I will have no reason to be ashamed of our poverty."

One Friday, a busybody next door noticed the smoke.

I did not see the rabbi or his wife buy food this week, let alone flour, she thought, *so how can they be baking bread?*

She was in the middle of making her own bread, but being such a nosy busybody, she had to see her neighbors' bread for herself.

Putting aside her dough, she knocked with a demanding rap-rap-rap on her neighbors' door.

Hanina's wife heard the loud rapping. She was too embarrassed to open the door. She hid in the bedroom instead, trying to pretend she wasn't home.

What did the nosy busybody do? She opened the door, boldly walked inside, and looked in the oven. The oven was filled with baking bread!

"The bread is getting puffy. Where is everyone? Why don't they come home and watch over their baking bread?"

As the loaves started to turn brown, she rushed to the door. "Come home!" she shouted. "Your bread is going to burn!"

She rushed to the window. "Quick, quick! Your bread is burning! Bring a shovel!"

When she turned around, Hanina's wife was already there, a long paddle in her hands, calmly removing the loaves from the oven.

"A miracle," said Hanina's wife.

"Yes, indeed. It's a miracle I got here just in time," said the busybody. "If I hadn't, your bread would have burned. Now, thanks to me, it's perfect—puffy and golden brown."

"Bread is always miraculous, isn't it?" Hanina's wife said, offering her neighbor a puffy, golden brown loaf. "It's so fragrant and filling."

"And it's especially miraculous," she added quietly, after her nosy neighbor had left, "when it's made from twigs."

Though she is never identified by name, Hanina Ben Dosa's wife, like her husband, was known for her wisdom and piety.

In those days, her husband's prayers were famous for bringing on the rain and curing the sick, but one Friday a prayer appears to have been answered—before it was ever made! And what was that unstated prayer? Was it for bread? Or was it a prayer for something as important as bread?

I'd like to think that a neighbor who had bread for the Sabbath would share it with her less fortunate neighbors, instead of trying to humiliate them the way the nosy busybody tried to humiliate Rabbi Hanina and his wife. So, to this story from the Babylonian Talmud (*Ta'anit,* 24b–25a), I added one more ingredient—which of course requires one more question. Why would Rabbi Hanina's wife share the miraculous bread with such a bad neighbor?

The Observant Cow

What a cow! So good-tempered and hardworking.

The Sabbath-observant Jew who owned her worked hard, too, six days a week. On the seventh day he rested, and so did his cow. To celebrate God's day, the man gave his cow an extra portion of hay.

Alas, one year the observant Jew fell on hard times, and he could no longer afford to keep a cow, even a good-tempered and hardworking one. He was forced to sell her.

A Gentile bought the cow from him and put her to work.

The cow worked just as hard for her new master as her old, but on the seventh day, despite her new master's insistence, she refused to work.

"Get up, Cow," he said. "It's time to plow."

The cow wouldn't get up.

"Get up, Cow," he shouted. "Right now!"

The cow wouldn't get up.

"Get up, Cow," he yelled, and he beat her: <u>POW!</u>

The cow cried, "Mooooo," but still she wouldn't get up.

The fellow ran to fetch the cow's former owner. "Look here," he said, "there is something wrong with the cow you sold me. She refuses to move. She's lazy and good-for-nothing. I want my money back!"

The Jew saw that the observant cow did not want to work on the Sabbath, so he leaned over and whispered in her ear, "Dear Cow, when you worked for me, we did celebrate the Sabbath. But now that you work for a non-Jew, you can no longer observe God's day. So please, be a good cow and do as he wishes. Get up now and pull the plow."

The cow obeyed.

The cow's new owner was amazed. "I beat the cow but she wouldn't move," he said. "You only had to whisper in her ear and she moved. Are you a wizard?"

"No," said the Jew, "I am not a wizard. Let me explain. The cow used to celebrate the Sabbath to honor the seventh day, just as God commanded. I merely told her that you were now her master and that even though you do not observe God's commandment, she must do as you wish."

The man listened carefully and asked himself, "If a <u>cow</u> does as God commands, how can I, made in the image of God, do any less?"

After that, he too became an observant Jew. And since it was a cow who led him to study the Torah, he was called Yochanan Ben Torta, "Yochanan, Son of the Cow."

The son of the cow gained fame as a scholar.

And the cow? She's famous, too, because this is, after all, <u>her</u> story, told and retold from then till now.

What a cow!

"Torta" is the Aramaic word for cow. Aramaic is an ancient language that was spoken by the peoples of Syria and Upper Mesopotamia—and by the Jews, too, after they were exiled to Babylon in the sixth century B.C.E. As the everyday language, it was used in the writing of many texts, including parts of the Bible and much of the Talmud. Aramaic prayers are still recited today, such as the *Mourner's Kaddish* and familiar sections of the Pesach seder.

Yochanan Ben Torta was a great sage like his colleague Rabbi Akiva (*see* "Everything for the Best"). They both tried to find lessons in the Romans' destruction of Jerusalem, left in ruins in 70 C.E. For example, Rabbi Ben Torta taught that hatred of one's fellow man is as bad as idol worship or bloodshed.

One man's life was changed by a cow—so says this midrashic tale from the *Pesikta Rabbati,* 14. But if some practical person says, "That cow was only a creature of habit," what would *you* say? Can animals teach people important lessons about life? Is the cow really the star of this story? Or is it the Sabbath-observant Jew? Could the star be the convert himself—the man who becomes Ben Torta?

The Hat
in the Fish

Joseph was a poor man, but he didn't worry about his poverty. As long as he earned a few coins each week he could honor the Sabbath like a rich man.

Each Friday night, he'd bathe, wash his hair, and put on fresh, clean clothes. He'd cover his rickety old table with a white cloth, set out two Sabbath candles, and feast on fresh fish and wine. His neighbors called him Joseph the Sabbath Man.

One of Joseph's neighbors was as rich as Joseph was poor, but he always worried about his wealth. He was afraid he might become poor someday. *It would be terrible,* he thought, *to be as poor as my neighbor, Joseph the Sabbath Man.*

The rich man consulted fortune-tellers, hoping that their predictions could help him protect his wealth. To his dismay, a fortune-teller from Chaldea told the rich man something truly frightening.

"Joseph the Sabbath Man," announced the Chaldean, "will consume your wealth."

What? How can Joseph do that? wondered the rich man. But he was so frightened by the fortune-teller's strange prediction that he sold all his land and property. With the money he received he bought large and valuable jewels, which he sewed into his hat for safekeeping.

But none of the fortune-tellers he had consulted warned him about crossing a river on a windy day.

One such day, when the rich man crossed a river, a gust of wind blew his hat off and carried it downstream.

"My hat! My hat!" he cried, leaning over the edge of the ferryboat, arms outstretched. "Stop the boat!"

No one could understand why he'd gotten so excited about a lost hat. Surely such a rich man could buy another hat. A hundred hats! Besides, even if the ferry could stop, the hat—as anybody could plainly see—was already sinking beneath the surface of the water.

Mistaking the hat for a smaller fish, a big fish swallowed it.

Later, a fisherman on the riverbank noticed a big fish swimming slowly, dragging its fat belly in the riverbed. He caught the fish with one quick toss of his net and threw it into a basket with the rest of his catch.

He set down his basket in the marketplace. "Fresh fish for sale," he called. "Who will buy my fresh fish?"

"Show that big one to Joseph the Sabbath Man," a woman told him. "Joseph always buys fresh fish for the Sabbath."

"It's a fine fish," Joseph agreed, "and heavy, too. I'll take it," he said, handing the fisherman his last hard-earned coins.

When Joseph cut the fish open, he was disappointed. "It's not the fish that's heavy," he said, "it's this hat full of stones. And not only are they heavy, they're sharp. And not only are they sharp," he cried, picking one up carefully between two fingers, "they aren't stones. They're jewels!"

Having no use for such large and valuable jewels, he sold them for 13 piles of gold coins.

Joseph knew exactly how he'd spend his new-found wealth. He'd honor his Sabbaths with the best that money could buy: the tallest candles, the softest bread, the sweetest wine, and, of course, the freshest fish, with or without a belly full of jewels.

The scholars who compiled the Talmud gave much thought to how people on the Sabbath should behave. They wrote pages and pages about ways to honor the holy day of rest. "The Hat in the Fish" is a folktale that was included in the Talmud for the values it teaches—loving and celebrating the Sabbath being one of the most important.

In its original version, this story from the Babylonian Talmud (*Shabbat,* 119a) concludes with the saying, "He who lends to the Sabbath is repaid by the Sabbath itself."

Does this mean that those who honor the Sabbath will find riches in lost hats? If they do not find hats filled with jewels, what riches will they find on the Sabbath? And speaking of riches, if you happened to be rich in material things, would you keep all your wealth in one hat?

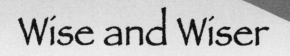

Wise and Wiser

76

When the two wise men of Athens saw the little rabbi with the ugly face, they couldn't help but wonder, "Is <u>this</u> the famous wise man of Jerusalem?"

"Look at his fingernails. They're dark with soot," one of the Athenians said. His own fingernails were spotless. "He must burn charcoal for a living."

The other, feeling superior to a lowly charcoal burner, said, "Before we ask him any really important questions, let us test his so-called wisdom."

So the wise men of Athens brought two eggs for Rabbi Yehoshua's inspection. "Can you tell us," they asked, "which one of these eggs comes from a white chicken and which one comes from a black chicken?"

Rabbi Yehoshua Ben Hananiah didn't answer right away. Instead he presented the wise men of Athens with two cheeses. "First," he said, "can you tell me which one of these cheeses comes from a white goat and which one comes from a black goat?"

The wise men of Athens whispered to each other.

"Do you know?"

"No, do you?"

Neither of them knew, so the first said, "Let us talk no more of eggs and cheese. Eggs and cheese are not as important as salt. Salt is essential for life."

"Can you tell us," asked the second, "how we can keep salt from spoiling?"

Rabbi Yehoshua nodded his head. "Of course. A mule who has given birth to a baby mule must stand guard over it."

The wise men of Athens pondered this response. "But Rabbi, how can such a mule guard the salt? Mules never give birth."

Answered the rabbi, "How true that is! And salt never spoils either."

The wise men began to wonder: Was Rabbi Yehoshua wiser than they thought, or was he a joker? He had a little smile on his face, so they couldn't be sure. They decided to ask him a more serious question.

"Can you tell us, Rabbi, where the middle of the universe is located?"

Rabbi Yehoshua pointed up with his finger and answered, "Right here."

"How can you prove it?" asked the wise men.

"Bring ropes and take the measurements for yourselves," replied the rabbi.

What a job! How and where would they begin? The wise men decided, for now, to trust the rabbi's measurements and went on to ask him another, more difficult question.

"Rabbi," they said, "can you tell us how to build a house in midair?"

"I will look for a suitable spot," he replied.

Rabbi Yehoshua said a holy name—and up he flew into the air, around and around, like a bird searching for a nest.

"I found a suitable spot," the rabbi called down, as he circled high above the wise men. "If you hand me bricks and mortar, I won't need to tell you how to build a house. I will build it for you myself."

"You're too high up," the wise men complained. "We can't reach you."

"Well," said the rabbi, "then how can we build?"

The wise men of Athens gazed up at the rabbi. He floated like an angel in the sky.

"Rabbi, Rabbi, please come down," they begged. "We have only one more question."

In an instant, the rabbi, with a big smile on his face, stood beside them.

"Can you tell us what is truly important in life?" the wise men asked the rabbi, who now seemed almost beautiful to them and not ugly at all.

"Friends are truly important, so make a good friend," said the rabbi. "You can ask as many questions of a friend as you like, and stay up a thousand nights together discussing the answers." The smile on his face grew even wider.

And the wise men of Athens smiled back.

Rabbi Yehoshua Ben Hananiah lived in the end of the first and beginning of the second century C.E. and was known for his intelligence, sense of humor, and ability to help settle disagreements. As for his appearance, he was said to be short and ugly.

In the Babylonian Talmud (*Bekhorot,* 8b), the wise men of Athens ask the rabbi several "test" questions. For this story, I selected four of those questions and made up the fifth. However, the answer to that last question—about what is truly important in life—comes from one of the rabbi's own teachings: "Make a good friend." These words are from the "Ethics of the Fathers" *(Pirke Avot),* one of the most popular parts of the Talmud.

Rabbi Yehoshua wins over the Athenians with his warmth, wit, and common sense, but he also questions the meaning of wisdom. Can wisdom be measured with a test? And can a good answer to a silly question—or a silly answer to a good question—reflect wisdom?

Rabbi Nachman of Breslov (1772–1810 c.e.) taught that when Rabbi Yehoshua said the middle of the universe is "Right here," he meant, "When a person does a good deed, a blessing descends from above." Through the ages, renowned teachers like Rabbi Nachman have interpreted and reinterpreted each word of the Talmud, expanding the sea of knowledge ever wider and deeper, answer by answer, question by question.

About these words . . .
Definitions

—for readers young and not so young, who would like to learn more*

Aramaic–Aramaic (ar-ah-MAY-ick)
An everyday language spoken by Jews of long ago, written using the Hebrew alphabet. Much of the Talmud is in Aramaic, as well as several well-known prayers. Certain Jewish documents, such as marriage contracts, are still written in Aramaic. In some small Middle Eastern communities, Aramaic remains a spoken language, even today.

Athens–English (ATH-enz)
A flourishing city-state in ancient Greece and now capital of the modern nation. Athens came under Roman rule in 146 B.C.E. and fell to the Goths (a Germanic people) in 267 C.E.

Babylonian Talmud–English (Baa-beh-LO-nee-an) and Hebrew (TAHL-muhd)
The most commonly studied version of the Talmud. In 135 C.E., the Roman Empire, which ruled the Land of Israel, killed vast numbers of Jews or sold them into slavery—as punishment for their numerous uprisings. Many rabbis managed to escape and went to Babylon. There, in the sixth century C.E., rabbinical scholars finished the Babylonian Talmud, in which

*Compiled by Janet Greenstein Potter

84

they wrote down the accumulated knowledge of the Jewish people. (*See* Talmud; *see* Jerusalem Talmud.)

Bar Kochba–Aramaic (BAR KOKH-bah)
"Son of a Star," an Aramaic name bestowed upon Shimon Ben Kosiba by the great Rabbi Akiva. Bar Kochba was the leader of the Jews' last major rebellion against the Roman Empire, which took place in the Land of Israel from 132–135 C.E. The Romans defeated the Jewish warriors, and Bar Kochba died in battle. (*See* Romans.)

B.C.E.–English (BEE-CEE-EE)
An abbreviation used by Jews for marking dates that occurred "Before the Common Era." (*See* C.E.)

Bekhorot–Hebrew (bekh-or-OTE)
The word itself means "firstlings." *Bekhorot* is a section of the Talmud that discusses laws concerning firstborn animals and humans. (*See* Talmud.)

Berachot–Hebrew (b'ra-HOTE)
The word itself means "blessings." *Berachot* is a section of the Talmud that discusses various prayers and blessings. (*See* Talmud.)

carob–English (KER-ub)
An evergreen tree with glossy leaves. Carob fruits are dark-

brown, leathery pods, sometimes 10 inches long. They contain a sweet pulp with a flavor similar to chocolate.

c.e.–English (CEE-EE)
An abbreviation used by Jews for marking dates in the "Common Era." The Common Era is a time period that started more than two thousand years ago and continues today. (*See* b.c.e.)

Chaldea–Aramaic (cal-DEE-ah)
An ancient country in a region once called Babylonia (Baa-beh-LO-nee-aah), between the Tigris (TYE-griss) and Euphrates (you-FRAY-tees) rivers. Today this land is in southern Iraq (ih-RACK).

fig–English ((FIG)
A small roundish fruit with a wide, flat bottom and a pointed, narrow top. Figs have slightly wrinkled skin that is either brown, purple, green, yellow, or black. A ripe fig is soft and perishable. Growers often preserve figs by drying them, similar to the way grapes are turned into raisins.

Galilee–Aramaic (GAL-eh-LEE)
The hilly northern region of the Land of Israel. The word itself means "circle."

Gentile–English (JEN-tyel)
Anyone who is not Jewish.

Israelites–English (IZ-reh-lights)
The ancient term for the Jewish people descended from
the 12 tribes of "Israel," which is the biblical name for the
patriarch Jacob. (*See* patriarchs.)

Jerusalem Talmud–English (je-RU-se-lem)
and Hebrew (TAHL-muhd)
The first version of the Talmud to be completed. It was written
by rabbinical scholars living in the northern part of Israel,
who named this Talmud after their longed-for, beloved city
of Jerusalem. The Jews were banished from Jerusalem after
they revolted twice against the Roman conquerors. For
centuries, rabbis had preferred that Jewish knowledge be
handed down only through conversations between teacher
and student. But with the deaths of so many teachers during
the failed revolts, concern grew that this knowledge would be
forgotten if it were not written down. The Jerusalem Talmud
was completed in the fifth century C.E (*See* Talmud. *See*
Babylonian Talmud.)

Judea–English (joo-DEE-ah)
A kingdom in the southern part of ancient Israel. It was
named for Judah, one of the 12 tribes of Israel. Jews returned
to the region after the Babylonian exile. Judea is where the
Maccabees (MACK-ah-bees), a band of Jewish revolutionaries,
lived in the second century B.C.E.

Kohelet Rabbah–Hebrew (co-HEL-et rab-BAH)
A collection of stories, or *midrashim*, explaining teachings
found in Kohelet, which is part of the Bible. Kohelet is Hebrew
for preacher or assembler, as in "a person who assembles
wise sayings." The Greeks gave Kohelet a different title—
Ecclesiastes (eh-KLEE-zee-AS-tease), the name many people
use today. According to tradition, Kohelet, or Ecclesiastes,
contains the writings of King Solomon. It is the place in the
Bible where we find the famous saying, "For everything there
is a season, and a time for every purpose under heaven."
(*See* midrash.)

Lag ba-Omer–Hebrew (LOG bah-OH-mare)
A minor holiday that comes 33 days after Pesach. Some
scholars say Lag ba-Omer marks a military victory. Others
say it marks the end of an ancient plague. No one is really
sure. Many Jews gather together on Lag ba-Omer to honor
the memory of Rabbi Shimon Bar Yohai. They traditionally
celebrate with bonfires, hikes into the country, and sporting
events using bows and arrows.

Meron–Hebrew (may-ROHN)
An ancient village in mountainous northern Israel. For
centuries it was a great center of Jewish learning. Today,
people make pilgrimages to Meron to visit the tombs of
several renowned rabbis, including Shimon Bar Yohai. The
ruins of an early synagogue—partly carved out of rock—

stand nearby. A modern settlement called Meron has been founded on the site of the old village.

midrash–Hebrew (MID-rahsh); plural,
midrashim (MID-rah-SHEEM)
A story about laws, customs, or rituals of Jewish life mentioned in the Torah. The word comes from the Hebrew for "explain." Some midrashim are detailed discussions. Some are similar to fables. Others are like sermons with a moral. The entire body of work is called the Midrash. The earliest volumes, written in the Land of Israel, date from the second century C.E. Scholars continued to produce collections of midrashim as late as the 12th century, in places such as Greece, Italy, and France. Even today, works are being created in the midrashic style. (*See* Torah.)

Mourner's Kaddish–English (MORE-nerz) and
Aramaic (KAH-dish)
Kaddish is a prayer of praise to God. It has different forms. *The Mourner's Kaddish*—also known as the *Orphan's Kaddish*—is said when mourning for one's parents or other relatives, and on the anniversary of their deaths. It is recited at the graveside, in the mourner's home, and in the synagogue. The language of the *Kaddish* is Aramaic (ar-ah-MAY-ick). The word has its origins in the Hebrew word for "holy." *The Mourner's Kaddish* actually makes no mention of death; rather it speaks of God's greatness. (*See* Aramaic.)

mule–English (MYOOL)
An animal that can only be created by mating a donkey with a horse. A mule makes a unique sound—a combination of a horse's whinny and the bray of a donkey: "Whinnee-aw-ah-aw." Mules are intelligent and—despite their reputation—not really stubborn.

patriarchs–English from Greek (PAY-tree-arks)
The "founding fathers" of Judaism: Abraham, Isaac, and Jacob. As models for the Jewish people, each is associated with a special quality: Abraham with kindness; Isaac with justice; and Jacob with compassion—which means caring about people and trying to make those who suffer feel better.

Pesach–Hebrew (PAY-sakh)
The Hebrew name for the eight-day spring holiday of Passover. The festival celebrates the Israelites' exodus from ancient Egypt, where they had been slaves for four hundred years. Pesach begins with a long family meal and service, which together are called a "seder." (*See* seder.)

Pesikta Rabbati–Aramaic (peh-SEEK-tah rah-BAH-tee)
Part of the Midrash. A *pesikta* (plural: *pesiktot*) is a type of midrash or sermon, based upon verses from the Bible. *Pesiktot* are concerned principally with the Sabbath and holidays. *Pesikta "Rabbati"* means the "Great" *Pesikta*, one of the later midrashic collections, dating from the ninth century C.E. (*See* midrash.)

Pirke Avot–Hebrew (peer-KAY ah-VOTE)
A part of the Talmud that discusses moral and ethical behavior. The English translation is "Ethics of the Fathers." *Pirke Avot* contains quotes, general truths, and popular sayings from ancient Jewish sages and scholars. (*See* Talmud.)

pomegranate–English (PAH-meh-graa-net)
A big reddish berry, about the size of an orange, with a thick leathery skin. It has many seeds and a tart flavor. Pomegranates are one of the "Seven Species"—seven staple foods consumed by Jews in the biblical Land of Israel. The other six are olives, grapes, wheat, barley, figs, and dates.

Romans–English (ROH-menz)
Citizens of the ancient Roman Empire, which was centered in the city of Rome—today the capital of Italy. The huge Roman empire stretched from the Middle East to Britain, and from western Germany into North Africa. The language the Romans spoke was Latin. Their army was very powerful and conquered many nations. At the direction of their emperors, Romans built cities, palaces, roads, temples, and "amphitheaters"—large arenas used for contests and spectacles. After more than a thousand years, in 476 C.E., the main part of the empire collapsed when Rome was conquered by barbarians. The rest of the empire lasted another thousand years.

Sabbath–English (SAA-beth)
The seventh day of the week, observed by Jews from Friday evening, when the sun goes down, to Saturday evening, when three stars are visible in the sky. The Sabbath is a sacred day, spent praying, reading, eating, and resting. The Hebrew word for the Sabbath is "Shabbat" (shah-BAHT).

Sanhedrin–Hebrew (san-HED-rin)
From the Greek term for "Council of Elders." In ancient Israel, the Sanhedrin was the supreme court of the Jews. Approximately 71 wise elders gathered together to write laws and make judgments. The court even had its own police force. The Sanhedrin continued to meet for several hundred years after the destruction of the Second Temple. Eventually the elders fled Jerusalem and went to northern Israel. The Sanhedrin disbanded in 425 C.E.

scorpion–English (SCORE-pea-ahn)
A distant relative of spiders, ticks, and mites. It has a long, narrow tail with a poisonous stinger at the tip.

Second Temple–English (SEH-kend TEM-puhl)
The most holy place of worship and sacrifice in ancient Israel. The Jews completed its construction in 515 B.C.E. on the site of the First Temple, which had been destroyed by the Babylonians. More than five hundred years later, in 70 C.E., the very large and magnificent Second Temple was destroyed by a Roman general named Titus, in response to the Jews'

unsuccessful "Great Revolt." The Western Wall in Jerusalem is revered today because it is a remnant of the "mount" (or base) of the Second Temple.

seder–Hebrew (SAY-der)
The traditional, ceremonial dinner of Pesach, a holiday known in English as Passover. Every participant at the seder uses a book called the "haggadah" (hah-GAH-dah), which means "the telling." The haggadah contains prayers, songs, and the story of the Israelites' escape from slavery in ancient Egypt. It also gives the order of the rituals and the meal. In fact, the word seder means "order." (*See* Pesach.)

Shabbat–Hebrew (shah-BAHT)
A section of the Talmud that discusses what activities are allowed and not allowed on "Shabbat," which is the Jewish Sabbath, the day of rest. (*See* Talmud; *see* Sabbath.)

Ta'anit–Hebrew (TAH-AH-neat)
A section of the Talmud that discusses laws about public or group fasting. In ancient Israel, these fasts were announced with great frequency. The purpose was to have people pray and fast together to avert disaster, such as drought or famine. *Ta'anit* comes from the Hebrew word for "affliction," but people use it to mean "fast." (*See* Talmud.)

Talmud–Hebrew (TAHL-muhd)
"Talmud" comes from the Hebrew word for "learn or study."
It is a collection of ancient writings related to the Torah. In
the Talmud are more than two-and-a-half million words, set
down more than fifteen hundred years ago. Previously, this
knowledge had been passed from one generation to the next
only by word of mouth. The Talmud explains every aspect
of Jewish life, including daily prayers, commandments, and
holiday celebrations. The rabbis wrote two versions
of the Talmud. The Babylonian Talmud is bigger, more
detailed, and more complex than the first version, which is
called the Jerusalem Talmud. (*See* Babylonian Talmud; *see*
Jerusalem Talmud.)

Torah–Hebrew (toh-RAH)
The first five books of the Bible. The origins of all Jewish
laws and beliefs, as well as the ancient history and sacred
traditions of the Jews, are found in the Torah. It begins with
the "Creation" of the world and ends with the death of
Moses—the biblical prophet, lawgiver, and great leader of
the Jewish people. "Torah" comes from the Hebrew word
for "instruction."

Va-yikra Rabbah–Hebrew (vah-YEEK-rah rah-BAH)
A collection of stories, or *midrashim*, explaining teachings found in *Va-yikra*, which is the third book of the Five Books of Moses—the Torah. The word "*Va-yikra*" means "He called." Among the things *Va-yikra* discusses are laws about Temple sacrifices in ancient days and rules for keeping kosher. The Greeks gave *Va-yikra* a different title—Leviticus (leh-VIT-eh-kus), the name many people use today. *Va-yikra*, or Leviticus, is the part of the Bible where we find the famous saying, "Love your neighbor as yourself." (*See* midrash.)